It's fun to draw
Princesses
and
Ballerinas

Mark Bergin

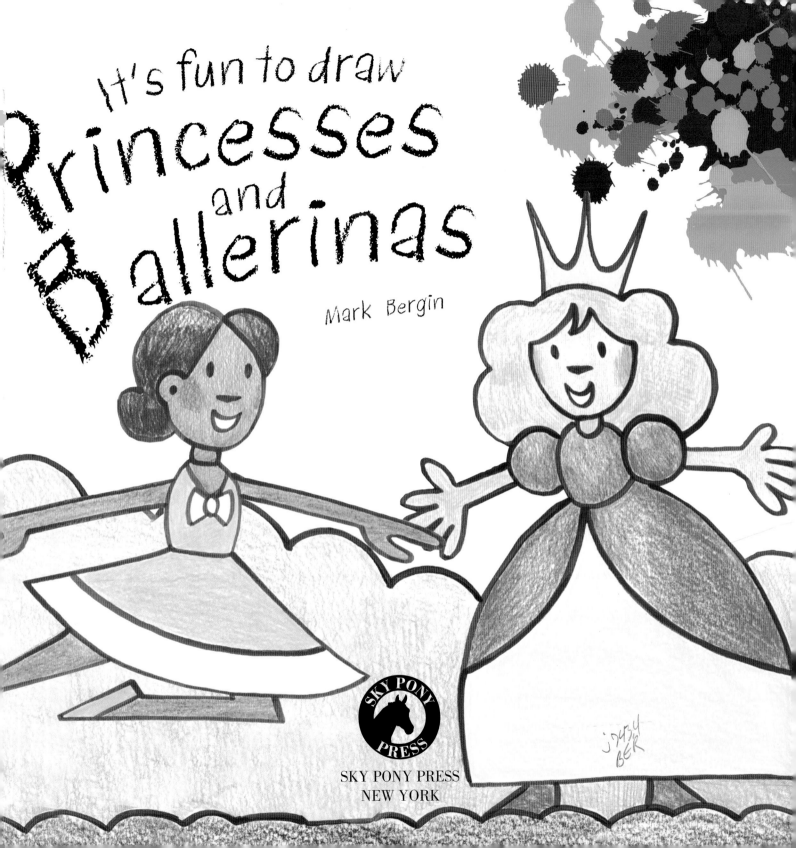

SKY PONY PRESS
NEW YORK

Mark Bergin was born in Hastings, England. He has illustrated an award-winning series and written over twenty books. He has done many book designs, layouts, and storyboards in many styles including cartoons for numerous books, posters, and ads. He lives in Bexhill-on-sea with his wife and three children.

HOW TO USE THIS BOOK:

Start by following the numbered splats on the left-hand page. These steps will ask you to add some lines to your drawing. The new lines are always drawn in red so you can see how the drawing builds from step to step. Read the "You can do it!" splats to learn about drawing and coloring techniques you can use.

Sky Pony Press books may be purchased in bulk at special discounts for sales promotion, corporate gifts, fund-raising, or educational purposes. Special editions can also be created to specifications. For details, contact the Special Sales Department, Sky Pony Press, 307 West 36th Street, 11th Floor, New York, NY 10018 or info@skyhorsepublishing.com.

Sky Pony® is a registered trademark of Skyhorse Publishing, Inc.®, a Delaware corporation.

Visit our website at www.skyponypress.com.

10 9 8 7 6 5 4 3 2 1

Manufactured in China, March 2012
This product conforms to CPSIA 2008

Library of Congress Cataloging-in-Publication Data is available on file.

ISBN: 978-1-61608-671-8

Contents

Princess Anna

Start with the head. Add a nose, mouth, and dots for eyes.

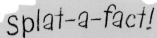

2 Add the arms and the top.

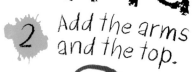

3 Draw in the hair and crown.

splat-a-fact!
Princesses often live in castles.

you can do it!
Use a felt-tip marker for the lines and add color using colored pencils. Use the pencils in a scribbly way to add texture.

3 Add the dress and the feet.

4

5

Louise

1 Start with the head.
Add a nose, mouth,
and dots for eyes.

2 Add the hair
and an ear.

you can do it!

Use a brown felt-tip
marker for the lines
and add color using
pencils.

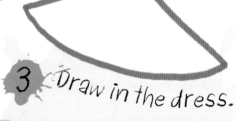

3 Draw in the dress.

splat-a-fact!

Ballerinas have to
work hard and
practice every day.

4 Add the arms and legs.

5 Add the dress details and a bow.

6

Henrietta

 1 Start with the head. Add a nose, mouth, and dots for eyes.

2 Add the hair.

you can do it!

Use crayons for all textures and paint over with watercolor paint. Use a blue felt-tip marker for the lines.

3 Draw in the tutu top and a big circle for the skirt.

4 Add the legs.

5 Draw the arms.

splat-a-fact!

Ballerinas can wear out 2 to 3 pairs of point shoes in one week.

9

Princess Margot

1 Start with the head. Add the nose, mouth, and dots for the eyes.

3 Draw in the arms and the feet.

you can do it!
Use crayons for all textures and paint over using colored inks. Sponge some of the inks for added texture.

2 Add the dress.

4 Add the crown and the hair.

5 Draw in the details of the dress.

Once upon a time a princess befriended a frog. Then the frog turned into a handsome prince!

11

Princess Lisa

1 Start with the head. Add a nose, mouth, and dots for eyes.

2 Add hair and a crown.

3 Draw in the top.

4 Add the arms and a handbag.

you can do it!

Use crayons for all textures and paint over with watercolors. Sponge some of the paint for added texture.

5 Draw the dress and feet.

Marina

1 Cut out the head and glue down. Draw on a mouth and a dot for the eye.

2 Cut out the tutu top and glue down. Cut out the skirt shape and glue down.

you can do it!

Start with a piece of colored paper for the background. Cut out shapes for the spotlight and floor. Glue them down. Now cut out all the shapes for the ballerina and glue them down in the order shown.

splat-a-fact!

A tutu can take about 60 to 70 hours to make.

4 Cut out the hair and glue down. Cut out the arms and glue down.

3 Cut out the legs and feet. Glue the legs down first, then add shoes.

MAKE SURE YOU GET AN ADULT TO HELP YOU WHEN USING SCISSORS!

Princess Helena

 1 Start with the head. Add a mouth and a dot for the eye.

 **2** Add the hair and crown.

 **3** Draw in three circles for the top.

Splat-a-fact!

Princesses appear in lots of fairy tales.

4 Add the arms.

you can do it!

Use crayons for the color and a blue felt-tip marker for the lines.

5 Draw the dress and feet.

17

Princess Melissa

1 Start with the head. Add a nose, mouth, and dots for eyes.

2 Draw in the dress.

3 Add the arms.

splat-a-fact!
Princesses don't usually do their own laundry.

you can do it!
Use a colored pencil for the lines and add color using watercolor paint.

4 Draw in the ropes and the swing. Add the feet.

5 Add the hair and crown.

18

19

Jennifer

1 Start with a head. Add a nose, mouth, and dots for eyes.

2 Add the hair.

3 Draw in the dress.

you can do it!
Add color using colored pencils. Use a black felt-tip marker for the lines, the shoes, and the pattern on the tutu.

4 Add the arms and legs.

5 Shade in the dress and shoes.

Splat-a-fact!
Ballerinas need to have strong ankles and knees.

20

Princess Nicole

1 Start with the head. Add a nose, mouth, and lines for eyes.

you can do it! Use a felt-tip marker for the lines and add color using colored pencils. Use the pencils in a scribbly way to add texture.

2 Draw in the top of the dress.

3 Add the rest of the dress.

splat-a-fact! Princesses need lots of mattresses.

4 Add the arms and feet.

5 Draw in the hair and crown.

Princess Heather

1 Start with the head. Add a nose, mouth, and dots for eyes.

2 Add the hair.

3 Add the hat and veil.

you can do it!

Use a green felt-tip marker for the lines and add color using watercolor paint.

splat-a-fact!

A princess has everything she wants—beautiful dresses, handbags, tiaras, and jewels.

5 Add the skirt and the feet.

4 Draw in the arms and sleeves.

Amanda

1 Start with the head. Add a nose, mouth, and dots for eyes.

2 Add the hair and ears.

you can do it!

Use a purple felt-tip marker for the lines and add color using colored markers.

3 Draw in the tutu.

4 Add the arms and legs.

splat-a-fact!

Dancing "en pointe" is performed by standing on the tips of your toes.

5 Finish off the details on the tutu.

Kirsten

1 Start with the head. Add a nose, mouth, and dots for eyes.

2 Add the hair.

3 Draw in the tutu.

you can do it!

Use a purple felt-tip marker for the lines and add color with soft, chalky pastels. Smudge and blend some of the colors to add texture.

splat-a-fact!

"Pas de deux" means a dance for two.

4 Add the arms and legs.

5 Finish off the details of the dress. Add a hairband.

28

Fiona

1 Start with the head. Add a mouth, nose, and a dot for the eye.

2 Add the hair.

3 Draw in the tutu.

you can do it!

Use crayons to add color and a blue felt-tip marker for the lines. Smudge or blend the color for more texture.

4 Add the legs.

5 Draw in the arms.

splat-a-fact!

It can take over 100 yards of tulle to make a tutu.

31

Index